More Than a Game
13 Keys to Success for Teen Athletes

Kyleigh Villarreal

More Than a Game

Copyright © 2016 by Kyleigh Villarreal

Cover Design By: MVP Publishing

Front/Back Cover Photographs: Samantha Toledo

For Bulk Orders: Please visit www.kyleighvillarreal.com

ISBN-13: 978-0692664247
ISBN-10: 0692664246
Printed in the United States of America

Dedication

This book is dedicated to my family, mentors and friends that have inspired me to live a life with purpose. I want to express a sincere heartfelt *"Thank You"* for inspiring and encouraging me to pursue my passion of sharing with others the life lessons that I have learned and continue to learn by playing a sport that I love so much. Without you believing in me and encouraging me this would still be just a dream.

Table of Contents

"A truly great mentor is hard to find, difficult to part with, and impossible to forget."

~Unknown

Foreword

Dear Reader,

I'm so excited for you. In your hand right now you are holding a wonderful gift.

What I love most about this book is it doesn't matter how old you are, what challenges you are facing or what sports you play...if you are someone with a dream, this book will give you the tools to make your dream a reality.

If you are looking for the steps to become a leader on your sports team, build confidence in yourself or be successful in life this book is for you. Kyleigh will take you by the hand and walk you through step by step how to make important choices on and off the playing field.

I first met Kyleigh when she was just 11 years old. I was hosting an online leadership class teaching the "*play-up principle*". The play up principle means to surround yourself with people who challenge you to be better, on and off the field.

I knew something was different about Kyleigh when she attended the same class three times! She was like a sponge, soaking in every point, asking questions and taking notes. What happened next in Kyleigh's life is one of the most

5

inspiring moments that I've ever witnessed. Kyleigh started applying the play up principle in her life.

She found ways to learn directly from the most successful athletes in the world. Despite facing great personal adversity, by the age of 12, Kyleigh had already become a published author, and successful softball player and motivational speaker!

Now while these things might not be your exact dreams, Kyleigh has unlocked a door to success and by using these keys shared in this book, you too could accomplish your dreams more quickly than you could ever imagine.

Kyleigh used the play up principle to learn directly from the best athletes and coaches in the world. These elite athletes that had reached a level of tremendous levels of success were pouring years of information and knowledge into Kyleigh.

This book packages up the best lessons she has learned from her mentors so you can know their secrets of success too.

I personally coach hundreds of girls across the US and Canada on how to become a leader and Kyleigh is the first young athlete I've seen really step into that role and create an opportunity for you.

She shares from her heart real life struggles of a 12 year old girl, who just wants to be the best athlete and leader she can be. Her stories will remind you how you don't have to be perfect to make a difference.

I believe by following these steps Kyleigh outlines, you too can go from living an ordinary life to an extraordinary life of impact.

On your Team,

Coach Jenn Starkey
Best Selling Author & Founder of MVP Leadership Academy

"Every accomplishment starts with the decision to try."

~Unknown

Introduction

My name is Kyleigh and I am twelve years old. Unlike my friends, I have lived with my grandparents since I was born. I have never known my mother and I have a father who is still trying to find his way in the world, which has not left a whole lot of time for me.

Looking back over the past few years some of these circumstances have made me look at my life a little differently. I think the most challenging was overcoming the fact that I was born with a disease called Recurrent Respiratory Papillomatosis (RRP) which produces reoccurring growths on my vocal chords and in my airway. Currently, there is no cure and will require no less than 100 surgeries in my lifetime. So far I have had 14 within the last 2 years.

In some ways it has made me feel like I was defective. No one could understand me, and I would get very frustrated. Nothing I would say was understandable to me or to anyone else. Almost a whisper.

It made me pull back from working towards my goals and dreams. Without having a voice, I felt like I was never heard, or taken seriously.

I was fortunate enough to get involved with sports, which taught me the importance of working together as a team. There we all were working together, each one of us with different strengths and weaknesses, trying to accomplish the same task. We all made mistakes, but we all figured out that we would learn from our failures. And in that process the failures made the successes that we had that much greater.

It was those lessons that helped me better understand my personal life. And over time, I realized that I have been blessed with people in my life that have come along side of me and have taught me that I have been given an incredible blessing; **the gift of choice.**

Every small thing that people said to me in order to make me feel better was said with a positive and caring attitude. They saw potential in me that I sometimes could not see for myself. Those were the things that impacted me the most. Guidance from coaches, mentors, teachers, family and friends.

I have always been raised in a family that has taught me that our circumstances do not define us. How we handle them does. My life will always be filled with things that are out of my control. And if I am not careful, I can become so focused on what I can't control that I lose sight of what I can.

By making the choice to surround myself with people that are positive and making wise decisions, I get to choose how I let those things that affect my life make an impact on me.

I have always known that I was created for a purpose. My great faith has proven that to me. Discovering that I can control how these little things affect my life I have discovered something about myself.

I am not defective. I am made for a purpose. And nothing is beyond achievement.

I have great dreams of playing college softball, and I am hopeful that one day I can play Olympic Softball. I know it takes lots of work and commitment. In fact I want to be a great pitcher like Monica Abbott, Cat Osterman or even Jennie Finch someday. By spending my time and energy on the things that matter, instead of the things that I can't control I can achieve great things.

You can choose to let your circumstances define you as a person, or choose to make your circumstances something that will inspire you to do greater things in your life.

Being an athlete is exciting, demanding and quite possibly the most rewarding time that you will ever experience. The lessons you learn on the field if applied will help you become a champion in sports and in life. This book has been created to help you become a better athlete and a more confident person so you can overcome any challenging circumstance to experience personal success.

Success begins by believing in yourself.

11

Building success is like building a house with your own two hands. Belief is your foundation. Once you have your foundation, you need specific tools and you will also need to know how to use them. When you don't know what tool to use for a specific job or how to use a specific tool, you find someone that does, and learn from them.

When you don't know how to do something in sports, you find people that do to help coach you. You can seek out coaches or players who become mentors because they have reached the success that you want to achieve.

Just as you would build a house using the tools made for the job, you begin to create a stronger self because you have surrounded yourself with positive influences providing solid direction and equipping yourself with the tools to succeed.

In this book, I will share with you ways to not only build confidence in yourself, but to share the positive energy with your teammates and friends that will help their performance as well. Through my personal experiences, I will show you ways that will help you determine the things that are important to you, rid yourself of the things that stand in your way and how to plan in a way to reach your dreams.

As you start this journey with me in reading this book, I want to tell you that every day I am blessed to still be learning lessons from the sport of softball. For you, it does not have to be softball. It's really about finding something that you are passionate about and the willingness to sacrifice to be the best you can at what you love.

For me, participating in sports taught me that while God-given abilities can be different for everyone, the one thing an athlete can control is their work ethic and attitude. Without that, none of these lessons would have been learned or applied in my life.

I was an average athlete that continues to work hard to maximize the abilities that God has given me. And through the hard work and dedication I am going to find every opportunity to grow and learn no matter what circumstances may arise in my future.

I challenge you to do the same!

Kyleigh

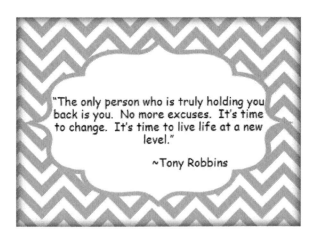

"The only person who is truly holding you back is you. No more excuses. It's time to change. It's time to live life at a new level."

~Tony Robbins

Chapter One

What's Holding You Back?

Have you ever wanted to do something, and you were afraid to do it because you thought that people would think it's really silly? I am one of those people. I begin to second guess everything as soon as I make a decision. Especially when I try to start something new.

Have you ever done that? Too many times I have caught myself thinking things like *"I'm not good enough"* or *"that's a stupid idea."* On the softball field I might say things like, *"I am never going to get that new pitch to work"* and shut down before I ever begin.

Sometimes it's easy to forget how amazing you really are! The fact is I know that I am not stupid, not all of my ideas are crazy and my efforts **are** good enough. If you find yourself lacking in belief, like I have, it might be time to call in reinforcements.

Surround Yourself With A Team That Believes In You.

Sometimes our friends or even family members actually create those fears and limitations that hold us back, or hold us down. They don't do this intentionally. Sometimes, they think they are just trying to protect us from failure. However, in order to grow, we need to experience failure too. That's how we learn. If you have a dream it's important to find a team that will believe in you and support you.

Sometimes it's just getting the right resources in place, getting the right kinds of mentors and people you can talk to and come along side of you to help give you that little hand up, the extra little push of motivation and encouragement that helps you fulfill your dreams.

Listen To Your Inner Voice

Until you find your success team, you have to listen to your *"inner-voice"*. It's that voice inside of you (*that nagging little voice*) that keeps reminding you of the things you dream about. It's the voice that whispers to you to take your dreams seriously and not letting your fears of failure take over.

We all have dreams and things that we want to accomplish. I believe that our ability to successfully work towards and reach our dreams often goes hand in hand with figuring out our purpose.

Everyone has a purpose in life. Our purpose is what allows us to grow and create and give back to others. All of us have been blessed with different gifts and abilities. To find our true purpose we have to be willing to get out of our own way. We must face our fears. I have to admit, I sometimes am my biggest obstacle.

Face Your Fears

One of my dreams is to be a successful softball pitcher. The other is to write books and share my stories with people. Every day, I work towards these dreams. There have been times on this journey when my negative thinking and the fear of failing to reach my dreams almost stopped me in my own tracks.

When I was confronted with a challenge and felt I was losing control of the situation, fear would creep in. Fear sounds like that voice that says *"I am not good enough."* That fear of failing was robbing me of my energy both creatively, physically and most importantly mentally. I would just shut down and give up. In softball, my pitching would suffer because I couldn't let a bad pitch or bad play go. It caused a ripple effect and soon the fear would take control of my beliefs, my choices and my results. My fear of letting others down became the very thing that was letting me and my own dreams down.

Whatever fear you have, whatever *"it"* is for you, it does matter. It matters because something inside is pushing you to the dreams you have. There is nothing wrong with wanting more than everyone else will settle for. Perhaps you don't want to be just a good pitcher on a select team. You might want to be the best collegiate pitcher in the state or top in the country.

I believe that when you want to accomplish something, fear is really a hunger pang for the need to grow. That inner voice, that nagging little *"hunger pang"* should always be taken seriously, it's either to protect you or to push you out of that

17

comfort zone to discover your purpose and to help you realize your dreams.

I am not saying that it never happens now and again, but I do know that it happens less. It is far easier now because I have been given the tools that help me make better decisions, I have people that support me in place that allow me to bounce ideas off of them and encourage me to grow, create and perform on the mound as well as in life.

It took looking towards others that I thought were successful, getting a mentor (in fact, several of them), having open communication with my coaches and family to help guide me in a direction that would be productive and get me out of the negative thinking and the fear of failing at my desired dreams.

Have Fun with the Challenge

Things don't always happen as you plan them. Sometimes there are setbacks. But you have to just move forward, get past the disappointment and *"Shake it off"*! Some of my fondest memories have been seeing my corners (1st and 3rd baseman) dancing and *"shaking it off"* - getting me to smile instead of focusing on a bad pitch. It was that silliness that helped me get refocused on the game instead of the misguided pitch. It made me relax, refocus and begin again.

Have a Game Plan

If you were going to face a tough opponent on a softball field, you would need to prepare a game plan. Fear is a tough opponent but if you track your progress you can beat fear too.

Recently I began the process of journaling. It has been one of my most powerful tools. I might write about what I read in my Bible, a dream I had last night, an experience I had yesterday, or what I hope to accomplish today. By writing it down, I could start to see a pattern of events that I quickly noticed affected my growth.

Journaling has helped me to:

- **Understand the Events of the Day**
  It's not just about what happens to me as much as it is the meaning I assign to what happens to me.

- **Clarify My Thinking**
  Writing it down helps me untangle my thoughts.

- **Notice My Feelings**
  I know feelings are not everything, but sometimes are a good indication something bigger is brewing that I need to address.

- **Connect With My Heart**
  I remember a passage from church
  Above all else, guard your heart, for everything you do flows from it. (Proverbs 4:23).
  It's hard to do if you lose touch with it.

- **Record Lessons Learned**

    I'm a better student and athlete when I am
    taking notes. Writing things down leads to better
    understanding. I write down what I want to learn,
    so I don't have to re-learn it later.

So far journaling has been one of the best personal development tools that have allowed me to grow. Sometimes when I write in my journal, it tends to be random thoughts and ideas. I may not have them all thought out at the time, but they are written down and when the time is right, I can get back to them once I have given the initial thought more consideration.

> "You can't give to others what you don't have, and you don't have what you don't take time to give yourself".
>
> ~Unknown

Recognize Fear for What It Is

Have you ever been so afraid of failing at something that you decided not to try at all? Or has a fear of failure meant that you undermined your own efforts to avoid the possibility of a larger failure? Many of us have probably experienced this at one time or another. The fear of failing can be paralyzing – it can cause us to do nothing, and make you afraid of moving forward. But when we allow fear to stop our forward progress in sports or everyday life, we're likely to miss some great opportunities along the way.

A few years back, I wanted to be on a specific team so bad, I practiced and trained like crazy awaiting the tryout opportunity. I was afraid stepping away from a team that I was comfortable with, to try out for a team that expected more and thought that it would be a good experience for me.

But when the day of the tryout came, I spent more time thinking about what could go wrong, that it crippled my efforts and quickly became the most embarrassing moment of my softball journey. At that point, I had to have a talk with myself. The point is, do not let your fears control the outcome. No matter how much you prepare, if you let self-doubt take over, it certainly will not miss the opportunity to defeat you.

To find the causes of the fear of failure, we first need to understand what "failure" actually means.

In questioning some of my friends, we all have different definitions of failure. A failure to one person can easily be a great learning experience for someone else.

All of us have some fear of failure. But failure is simply when we allow a fear to stop us from doing things that can move us forward to achieve our goals.

I could have easily stopped playing the game I love based on the performance at that tryout. At the time I felt so humiliated because I could not hit, catch or pitch that day. All because once the fear of failure took over, it was all consuming in every area. So what would failure mindset look like?

Typical signs would be:

- Being reluctant to try new things
- Self-sabotage by failure to follow through with goals
- Negative thoughts like *"I'll never be good enough"*
- Perfection and willingness to try only when you'll perform perfectly

Failure is a matter of perspective. It's almost impossible to go through life without experiencing some kind of failure. People who do so probably live so cautiously that they go nowhere. Put simply, they're not really living at all.

The wonderful thing about failure is that it's entirely up to us to decide how to look at it.

Redefine Fear in Your Life

We can choose to see failure as *"the end of the world,"* or as proof we just don't have what it takes. Or, we can look at failure as the incredible learning experience that it often is. Every time we fail at something, we can choose to look for the lesson we're meant to learn. These lessons are very important; they're how we grow, and how we keep from making that same mistake again. Failures stop us only if we let it.

Most of us will stumble and fall in sports and in life, and we can ultimately make some bad decisions in giving up. Think of the opportunities you'll miss if you let your failures stop you. Failure can also teach us things about ourselves that we would never have learned otherwise.

For instance, failure can help you discover how strong a person you are. Failing at something can help you discover your truest friends, or help you find unexpected motivation to succeed. Often, valuable lessons come only after a failure. Accepting and learning from those lessons is key to succeeding in life.

It's important to realize that in everything we do, there's always a chance that we'll fail. Softball statistically is a game of failure. Facing that chance, and embracing it, is not only giving you a courageous warrior mindset but allows us to have a more rewarding life with opportunity.

However, here are a few ways to reduce the fear of failing:

- **Practice a "What-if" Analysis**
  Most fear the unknown, so remove that fear by considering all of the potential outcomes of a decision you make. Example: If I practice pitching with dedication what will happen, and if I don't what will happen then?

- **Have a "Can-Do" Attitude**
  Think positive. Always. It's a powerful way to build self-confidence and remove the self-sabotage. Remove the word can't from your vocabulary altogether because it defeats you before you begin.

- **Learn it more than "One-Way"**
  Always have a plan "B" in place to help you feel more confident about moving forward. Think about two solutions of the task at hand, if one is not working, go to *"Plan B"*- but do not give up. Just because one way does not work, be open to trying something different until you succeed.

> **"If at first you don't succeed, try, try, try again!"**
> **~William Edward Hickson**

If you are still afraid and fear failure. We will attack those fears in the next chapter by setting goals. Goals will help define where we want to go and what we want to achieve. Taking one small step at a time will help build your confidence, keep you moving forward, and prevent you from getting overwhelmed with visions of your final goal.

It's important to realize that we always have a choice: we can choose to be afraid, or we can choose not to be. This is the power of your choices.

Make things that matter to you **matter.** Lose the fear of failure and the thought that you don't have the time. What you will find is that you'll make the time to create the life and the dream you work for. There is no need to fear failure. It's all a part of learning. You have to be willing to make mistakes, and if you fail when doing your best you can feel confident that you made them going hard at 100%. If we fail enough, we will attempt to do more to succeed because we want to do better.

> *"It's not because things are difficult that we dare not venture. It's because we dare not venture that they are difficult."*
>
> *~Seneca*

So "What's holding you back?" Starting now, I challenge you to think differently; be brave enough to change your mindset and make your dreams a reality.

"Set a goal so BIG that you can't achieve it until you GROW INTO THE PERSON THAT CAN."

~Unknown

Chapter Two

IF YOU DON'T HAVE A GOAL, YOU DON'T HAVE A GAME!

It seems that everyone always starts by asking if I have a goal, what's my goal or have I met my goal? In school my teachers give me goals, my coaches give me goals….even my family and not to mention my mentors. So I finally came to the realization that goals are important. It took me awhile to figure that out.

It doesn't matter whether you have small dreams or big expectations, setting goals will allow you to plan what you need to accomplish in order to get there, like a GPS roadmap.

Goals can be small achievements that can take a day to complete or a lifetime to accomplish. There's no doubt they are needed in order to create the roadmap to reach what you are trying to achieve.

Setting goals for yourself can really fuel your ambitions. It isn't just about creating a plan and holding yourself responsible. I think it's really more about accomplishing something that gives us inspiration and to aim for things that we never thought could be possible.

When I play softball we play many games. For my team, going to the Nationals is a big deal. We have to **earn** a berth into the games. It's not just about getting there, but doing our personal best as a team and placing is the ultimate goal. Getting there is a process that is worked on with every game and every practice

27

along the way. Realizing that you have to perform at practice the way you play at games. You have to *"Go Hard"* and *"Bring It"* every time.

So our coaches and team plan. Our training plan looks something like this:

- Strength and Conditioning
- Skill Training
- Hitting/Bat Speed
- Specialist Training (Infield/Outfield/Pitchers/Catchers-game and team skills)

Whatever your goal may be, I find that it is helpful to create **S.M.A.R.T** Goals. I learned about this method not only in school, but also from mentors as they have helped me establish goals for success over the past year. I believe that these will be helpful to you as well.

Set Smart Goals

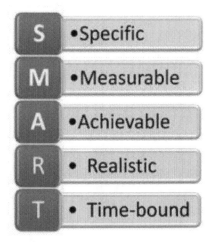

When setting goals you will find that specific goals have a much greater chance of being accomplished. But in order to get started you have to identify the areas that need to be worked on (the small goals), and then determine what is **S.M.A.R.T** about each one.

To give you an idea, let's try one out:

GOAL: Strength and Conditioning for Better Endurance

A general goal for this would be something like, "Get in better shape." But if you use the **S.M.A.R.T** method it would be something like, *"Go on a run every day after school",* or *"Do push-ups every night"* now that's a **SPECIFIC** goal.

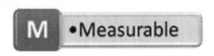

And since you have a specific goal in mind, you need to be able to measure it. You want this to be something that you have to stretch to achieve but also something you can build on over time. So let's say, *"I am going to run 1 mile every day after school",* and *"do 100 push-ups every night before going to bed."* Now you have something **MEASURABLE**!

Now that you set your goal, and have determined how you can get there you need to decide if there are any obstacles that will prevent you from being able to accomplish your goal. Perhaps it will require moving things around on your calendar or evaluating things to see if they are going to contribute to your desired success. If not, lose them.

It's important that you set tasks that help you reach the over-all goal. You can even set up several small goals that make the bigger goal **ACHIEVEABLE**. You don't have to make your goal so impossible to reach, so start small and work your way towards that goal. Better to have several small achievable goals than to never reach them at all. Progress is Progress.

how do you eat an
elephant?
one bite at a time

When you do work your way through the smaller goals that lead to accomplishing the larger goals, what seemed so far away and out of reach eventually moves closer, not because your goal gets smaller, but because you grow and excel to match them. One of the best benefits is that when you list your goals you build your self-image. And once you start making the effort, and see progress you will lose the fear and know that you had what it takes all along to meet your goals.

Perhaps this was one of the reasons that you felt you were being held back from reaching your dreams. By having goals and seeing the progress it satisfies the voice from within that gives you self-doubt and replaces it with, **"YOU CAN DO IT!"**

A goal that is **REALISTIC** must be one that you are both willing and able to accomplish. You are the only one who can decide high big your goal should be. Your goals should inspire you. If they don't, set new goals. Your goals need to be in alignment with your values. If there is a conflict between your goals and you, you won't achieve them.

If you know you can't stretch your capabilities enough to better your endurance through these goals, then you need to adjust so that you are working towards personal improvement that is achievable with hard work. Remember, *"Nothing worth having comes easy."*

Lastly, make the goals **TIME-BOUND**. With no time frame tied to the goal there is no sense of urgency. Do you think you would ever get the endurance to run 5 miles if you said to yourself, *"Someday I will run a mile after school"?* But if you create a timeline or deadline to the goal then you can set the plan in motion, even if it's just working your way to being able to run that mile.

It may start with "jog around the block", and becomes two blocks until you can run an entire mile. The point is that you are putting into motion working on the goal. The best goals have deadlines.

Writing in a journal is a great way to keep track of your progress. Checking in with yourself and recognizing your accomplishments towards your goals is the key to staying motivated, and if you fall behind (and that might happen) may even encourage you to work harder.

Sometimes it helps involving a friend. For me, when it comes to getting ready for the softball season and prepare for the goal of earning the berth for the National games I include my team or a team member like my catcher. She always motivates and keeps me on track. She will not allow me to make excuses, and we have a lot of fun challenging each other. Just because it is going to be work, doesn't mean it can't be fun!

It's also important to acknowledge when you have reached your goal. That means **CELEBRATE!!!!** Sometimes it is good to go back and look at how you reached the goal from beginning to end. See if you were happy with the timeframe, and if the goal was reasonable. It also may give you insights on things that got in your way and made it more of a challenge so that you can avoid those potential pitfalls on your next goal. (Like while making that run, don't stop and eat ice-cream because you pass the ice cream shop!)

Once you have completed the goal, you will want to continue to grow and set new goals for yourself. Before you know it, whatever your bigger goal was (mine being able to work with my team to earn a spot at Nationals) you will get to it sooner than you think is possible. Because at the end, it is true, " *if you don't have a goal you never get to the game*"!

So what is one of the things that you want to accomplish? Sometimes starting is the hardest part. But following a plan or a process like the **S.M.A.R.T** method, you will reach whatever goal you are trying to achieve. I don't know about you, but I am going to the game!

"If you fail to prepare, you prepare to fail."

~Mark Spitz

Chapter Three

PRACTICE AND PREPARATION

I am sure that you have heard the saying *"Use it or lose it"* especially when it comes to sports. In order to have success on the field you have to remember the importance of practice and preparation. Not only is it going to help you perform better at a game, but it is also a key element that allows for personal growth and improvement.

Practice sometimes can be the difference between yourself and your goals. Without practice, it can become the one key that is missing and become the very thing that will hold you back and leave you wondering why other teammates are so much better at *"that something"* you want to achieve. Practice is the one key that can make the difference between your performance being just good enough or being great on the field.

Practice is like a brutally honest friend. When you don't make a habit of making practice an important part of your training and make it a priority in your life, you are going to find yourself thinking you are not good enough and you want to kick that little friend called practice "OUT OF YOUR LIFE"! But don't. Preparation and practice is a great friend and will be there to help

35

build you up while you train and improve your skills. Practice, regardless of your sport, takes hard work, but not all hard work is practice.

Consider practice like this. Hard work is what you put towards a single task, it can be challenging and make you sweat and even bring you to tears. I have a friend that something as simple as jumping rope is her nemesis, mine is wall squats.

But when the hard work becomes something you do repetitively it becomes easier. Eventually it will be effortless and then the hard work becomes practice.

Have you ever worked really hard on something, only to find that the effort and hard work was just wasteful time and really did not show any results to what you were trying to achieve? I have and that is one of the reasons that you have to prepare in a way that makes all of the hard work matter. Stop wasting hours on things that are not making a difference. Practice and prepare like you're in the championship game.

> "The only way you should ever be able to tell it's a practice is by what you are wearing".
> ~Unknown

Practice, unlike hard work that sometimes can be meaningless, will never go unnoticed. When you practice consistently, it will eventually show regardless if you like it or not.

You get better, faster, and stronger and before you know it will push you forward to succeed.

Practice, when taken seriously, can be the beginning of some awesome experiences waiting to happen for you, for me or anyone willing to put into practice the time to build a skill and develop your talents, no matter if they are in sports or in life.

Practice is a key that will open the door to "your house", but not a minute sooner than you are ready for it. When you practice at anything consistently you will be rewarded. With it you gain a skill and loads of confidence.

Then the opposite is true when you don't practice. You lose your skills, perhaps not all at once but enough to make it really obvious and terrify or embarrass you back into practice. To give you an example: As you know, my favorite position on the field is a pitcher. I **LOVE** to pitch and I work hard at pitching. I go to my pitching coach every week and work on my skills and mechanics.

The weeks that I didn't put in the extra daily practices on my own it was definitely noticed. At first, it is frustrating but hardly bad enough to sound the alarm and I notice that what seemed so effortless, now takes so much more time and energy.

I begin to slip here and there and eventually I would lose my mechanics and the pitching skills that I had worked so hard for. The lack of personal commitment even for a short period of time was allowing my dream to slip right out of my hand, and the ball along with it. By allowing myself to *"slack off"* I was creating some bad habits and if I did not wake up to reality I was just losing the skill that I swore that I loved more than anything else.

Without practice you lose the sills that you have built. The less you practice, the faster it fades and it's a terrible thing to witness. Ask any coach. Mine lets me know, and makes me accountable for lack of practice. I am so appreciative that he lets me know and makes me responsible for my progress, or when I am falling behind because of the lack of practice and dedication.

Truth of the matter is that practice is a true friend.
- You can count on it
- You can schedule it
- You can plan it
- You can commit to it

And when you walk away you can always return to it as long as you believe in its power to get you to your goal.

The time you set aside to practice your sport is important. During practices, athletes work on their skills as well as encourage you to stay active and healthy while developing communication skills and building your self-confidence.

So when practicing anything, especially in sports, think to yourself...why do you play this sport? What drives you to want to get better? Sometimes I have found it very helpful to look up motivational quotes that help you out in times of frustration. One that I tend to repeat in my head is:

Truly dedicated athletes will seek out camps or clinics to improve their skills and use it as additional practices. Not because they have to, but because they choose to. Play with different people and push yourself to different levels of competition. You must be willing to step outside of your comfort zone. You can also attend special training events for other important goals in your life.

> "If it does not challenge you, it doesn't change you!".
>
> ~Fred DeVito

You can learn skills, but you'll never realize your full potential unless you practice. Don't just go through the motions. Strive to get better with each practice. Work as hard as you do when the coach is looking as when they're not. Be a good role model for others on the team. It's almost like wildfire. When others see you practicing hard and giving it your all it becomes contagious and before you know it everyone will pull together as a team and work harder.

Sometimes when you practice it will feel natural and easy when you are starting out, and other times, it may feel awkward or downright impossible. But remember the more you practice, the easier everything becomes. Over time, you will build muscle memory, and you are building up your mental and physical muscles as well. The more you practice the mechanics the easier it is to build from there.

I often read about those athletes that I admire and what inspires them to practice each day. I take their words of wisdom and allow it to inspire me, but don't be intimidated by their approach or process. They have spent thousands of hours at their sport, and continue to do so in order to stay on top of their game. We all have one thing in common, they all started at the same place we are.

I have always made it a point to ask those I admire this question.

"As a pitcher, what is the one piece of advice can you give me in this sport?" These are their responses:

Jennie Finch: "Never limit yourself, never be satisfied".

Monica Abbott: "One pitch at a time"

Cat Osterman: "If you look back at yesterday and think it was a big deal, then you haven't done anything today."

So if you find yourself asking if you are ever going to be as good as those amazing athletes, or those opponents that you face at any tournament that are challenging to you, there is only one way to level the playing field. When you are going up against athletes with more experience and that have great skills, the one thing *"the greats"* of this sport remind me of is that it is important to continue to grow your skills and talents.

There is only one way..........PRACTICE!

Practice is important for anything that you want to excel at. Be a friend to it, compromise it for nothing and it will get you to your desired goal whether it be on the field or beyond.

"There's a difference between interest and commitment. When you're interested in doing something you do it only when its convenient. When you're committed to something, you accept NO EXCUSES, ONLY RESULTS."
              ~Kenneth Blanchard

Chapter Four

COMMIT TO IT...HOLD YOURSELF TO YOUR WORD!

Commitment. Just the word alone tends to make you believe that you have to devote all of your time and energy to it. But I do not think that commitment has to be something that makes us afraid. I like to think that commitment is nothing more than a type of habit that you create. And good habits last a lifetime.

It's something that you promise yourself, an agreement that you make to accomplish that task or skill that you want to achieve. And if it's something that you have a passion for, it can't be that bad.

If you commit to the right things it becomes part of your life, and something that makes you feel like it's always been there. Anything that you want to achieve takes time, patience, effort and practice (yes, all of the keys work together). It takes self-discipline and a desire to reach whatever in life you are wanting to achieve.

Commitment is an agreement with yourself to work as hard as you can to reach your goal, but like some of the other keys, it takes work. It's the heart and soul in reaching your goals.

Choose Your Commitments Wisely

If I wanted to be a pitcher and never committed myself to practice, then I would never reach the goals I have set for myself, nor will you.

Commitment really is a way of saying, *"How bad do you want it?"* If you're committed, you'll find a way to make it happen. It is okay to have other interests but it is important to know if you are truly committed or just interested. If you have a big dream and goal it requires commitment.

Just to give you an idea of the difference between interest and commitment:

Interest	Commitment
* Random Postings on Social Media	* Reading about your sport
* When you Feel Like it	* Practice every chance you get
* Puts it off- Always another day	* Focus on Importance of Practice
* Makes Excuses	* Strives on improving skills

Don't be afraid to start. Sometimes I found myself thinking I did not know enough to make a commitment and just did not think I was ready. But the truth is that there will always be more to learn, and if you keep waiting until you are ready, you will never be ready to commit.

Once you make the agreement with yourself, you are going to learn more from just the fact that you started in the first place.

Commitment does not mean that you won't trip up sometimes. Sometimes when you make a commitment and you have found yourself getting off task it can sometimes be difficult to get going in the right direction again. Too often when I found myself at that place I realized that I was seeking "perfection" and could not mentally accept that I had failed and so I would move on to pursue a new something.

But hard work and commitment is a key to succeed. Hard work and dedication and commitment to your goals. Make the commitment to yourself in order to achieve your dream. Dedicate yourself to working hard to reach your goals, and most importantly; have fun while doing it!

Commitment & Kindness

My grandmother's rule is always to be kind to myself and others. My rule is to be firm with myself. The sweet combination is my key to commitment. I have many times and always with regret have dropped a commitment because it was hard. Making a commitment is practicing firmness and self-discipline when you are keeping your word on your commitments and also practicing kindness to yourself when you fall behind once in a while.

There are times when it really (*really*) is not your fault that a commitment is lost. There are days when simple things going on in your life throw you a curve ball and you have to step back and take care of something else. You have to accept that, and remember one thing, **you can start over**.

At the moment you are ready to go all out, know that it begins with your mindset. You have to decide that nothing is going to stand in your way of success. It's important for you to renew your commitment so that you refuse to let anything stand in the way.

Just remember, you have to have a goal. It's hard to commit yourself if it's just a dream without a finish line. So when you are ready to make the commitment, remember your S.M.A.R.T goals. The key to commitment is to have a vision that is so awesome you are willing to do anything to achieve it.

And while you are in the *"Go for it"* mindset, you have to bring your *"A-Game"*. Unfortunately, motivation sometimes is not enough. It might be enough to get started, but as soon as the work starts the enthusiasm slowly can begin to fade.

Making commitments is another area that working on S.M.A.R.T goals work well. When making commitments, I have a few things that I find helpful. They are:

- **Write Goals in Your Journal** (daily/weekly)
  Remember tracking the successes of the day

- **Tell others what you are doing**
  When your goals are open, family and friends will be supportive in helping you achieve them.

- **Involve Others with Similar Goals**

  By surrounding yourself with others, like teammates trying to accomplish similar goals, it will help motivate you and keep you committed.

If you have been putting off your commitments, ask yourself why? What are you waiting for? If you're waiting for the stars to align, or that perfect moment to start…Newsflash….**IT WILL NEVER COME.**

IF WE WAIT
UNTIL WE'RE READY
WE'LL BE WAITING
FOR THE REST OF
OUR LIVES.

There will always be a new problem that could potentially prevent or delay a commitment. You have to be willing to make an agreement with yourself. This agreement must be important enough so that you are willing to start immediately without exceptions. If you are truly dedicated, then you will make the task a priority so that you are able to accomplish the goal and be able to perform at your highest level. Dedication is simply the will to work and making it happen.

> *"COMMITMENT is the glue that bonds you to your goals."*
>
> ~Jeff Koening

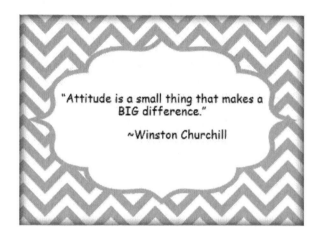

"Attitude is a small thing that makes a BIG difference."

~Winston Churchill

Chapter Five

ATTITUDE IS MORE IMPORTANT THAN SKILL

Sports are important to you. You have put a great deal of effort in each key area. With all of the training efforts you put your ego on the line every time you compete. After all, you have worked very hard, and so has the other team or members of your own team. When you don't play well, you become disappointed. I know personally that it does not feel well because you care about the sport you love, or you would not be there in the first place.

Sometimes there is a point that you can lose perspective and your feelings toward your sport can hurt the way you play, as well as bring the moral of a team down in the process.

A few months ago, I was struggling on the mound. I was being pulled from the game just after a few innings. I could not understand why. I had the skills and was a good pitcher. I hustled and practiced every day. But I was struggling that day. The coach did the right thing by removing me, because my mental attitude was showing all over my face and in my body language. The pitches were not going the way that I liked and I felt more helpless and powerless to change it. It made me feel defeated and angry.

The pressure I put on myself for not making the pitches as I wanted to make, with the accuracy that I knew I could deliver, was exhausting. I had nothing left. And, I did not want to be pulled from the mound and have someone take my place. And when they did, my attitude was not one that I was proud of. I felt like I had let everyone down, myself included. I just would not "*shake off*" the personal disappointment and not only did it zap my energy, it was affecting my teams spirit as well.

That game marks one of the worst – and –the best examples of how a bad attitude can turn an average situation into a terribly hopeless one, not to mention the stress it puts on you and your team.

I still get disappointed when I do not feel I have executed my pitches from the mound the way that I would have liked. But how I handle those disappointments are handled in a way that are more positive.

Have you checked your attitude recently?

You have to be more than an athlete with tremendous ability, great strength, and great understanding of the game. An athlete's attitude can make or break your ability to be successful on a team or in your life. The athletes that have the winning attitudes, who can take constructive feedback, care about the team more than themselves, who are positive and passionate about their sport. Those are the ones that succeed, not only on the field, but in life!

Having a positive attitude regardless of the sport you are in can and will improve your performance. If you play a sport your attitude is something that a coach or teammate will notice long before any skill that you have.

A positive attitude will bring you more confidence, whereas a negative one will affect your performance and morale within your team.

A negative attitude will affect your performance not only in sports, but in everything you do in life. When you feel negative try and turn that around by replacing whatever negative thought you are having with positive thoughts or images. When I pitch and mess up, I step back before the next pitch and take a second to close my eyes and visualize a great pitch. It may not happen every time, but the more you can picture success on the mound over time you will become more confident and then the misguided pitches will not affect you as much.

Just remember, don't be so hard on yourself. Sometimes having a good sense of humor can help you deal with any problem and can improve your attitude. When my team *"shakes off"* the bad play, we all start laughing and smiling. We relax, I relax and the overall attitude changes for the better.

It is also helpful to have relationships with people that have positive attitudes. It makes a big difference when spending time with people that are always negative. Over time, you also see the negative in everything. But if you search out people that always see the better side of life it helps you maintain your own positive attitude.

Here are some helpful ways to ensure your attitude stays upbeat:

- **Always Face the Day With Purpose.**
  Everything you do needs to serve a greater goal. Don't waste time and energy on things that really don't matter.

- **Always Strive to do More Than Required**
  Doing the same old thing every day gets depressing after a while. So take the time to change up the routine a bit. And stretch to do a little more. When you increase accomplishments, it has its own way of making your attitude of accomplishment that much sweeter.

- **Find Friends That Share a Positive Attitude**
  Make it a point to surround yourself with friends and people that are positive and remove yourself from those that seem to constantly complain and see the negative in situations. It will make a huge difference on how you approach your day.

- **Laugh At Yourself. Don't Take Everything So Seriously.**
  Be able to laugh at everything, if you can. People that laugh at your short comings will lose the power they have

over you when making mistakes.

- **Don't Judge the Limitations of Others**
  I used to judge those that I did not feel put in the same amount of time I did. It really affects your own attitude. So let them worry about themselves, don't make yourself miserable because others don't share the same passion that you do. What you will find is that by leading by example, away from the drama, soon others will want to follow your example, and set higher standards and goals for themselves.

- **Have an Attitude of Gratitude**
  Just remember to say *"thank you"*. Always thank those that help you, a team mate, a coach, a friend. When you have a positive attitude and are grateful to those that spend their time and sharing their knowledge with you it creates an appreciative attitude and relationship. No matter how hard a coach is on you, always thank them at the end of practice. It creates an attitude of appreciation and lets others know that you appreciate their time.

Having a positive attitude makes people want to spend time with you. And by you having a good attitude not only will you excel in your goals and dreams but it will encourage others to do the same. More importantly, what would be the point of being successful in your dreams and goals if you're always feeling lousy?

Attitudes Are Contagious

Equally important is the people that you choose to spend your time with. If you surround yourself with those that always complain and whine and have a bad attitude, it will eventually affect you. Rather than investing all of the emotional energy trying to change them, you're probably better off looking in the mirror and changing yourself. It's your attitude that creates positive change in your life.

The mindset that we have towards playing our sport and in everything that we do reveals our mental attitude. A positive attitude is needed to be successful, both on and off the field.

It's really easy to get mad at a bad play or bad call, and it's easy to point fingers and assign blame. But that type of frustration starting with one teammate can easily spread throughout the team.

The good news is that a good attitude is just as contagious as a bad attitude. You can possess great skills and it be overlooked with a bad attitude. You must make a personal decision every day to be positive whether it be at home, at practice, at games or at tournaments.

Don't let a bad attitude be the thing coaches, teachers and friends remember you by. Don't let the negatives be the thing that defines you and follows you. Believe in yourself, in your abilities, and in your training. And when you feel the negative…*"Shake it off"*.

ATTITUDE IS EVERYTHING!

"The good and the great are only separated by their willingness to sacrifice."

~Kareem Abdul-Jabbar

Chapter Six

EXCELLENCE WITHOUT EXCUSES

Successful athletes understand that without hard work you get nowhere in sports. It's a lot like basic science of life: your input will equal your output.

> Disciplined Effort:
> What you do every day matters
> more than what you do every
> once in a while.
>
> *By Jason Lewis*

You simply cannot depend on luck to get you anywhere. However, you can always depend on the skills and ambition to get you wherever you want to be.

An athlete is willing to sacrifice everything to earn their position and will eat and sleep thinking about the game. It becomes a part of their life and even if they have to miss being with friends or up early to exercise before school starts everyday they make sure that they do it because they love it.

They will rarely complain about how hard they are working because they know that all of their hard work will pay off. They expect the most from themselves, and when they are focused, there is nothing that can stop them.

Achieving excellence is something that we all want. But if it was so easy, everyone that wanted it would have it. Excellence is like an exclusive club in my opinion. A handful of people do some amazing things and they are the leaders of our sports, in our schools and in our life that we look up to.

Some just get lucky, because they are at the right place at the right time. I had an experience like that when I first started playing softball. I was 8 years old and never even had a glove before I joined the team. Luckily they needed a player. The team was amazing, and most of the girls had been on this team since T-Ball. But I wanted to play more than anything. So I played every day until I could catch and throw the ball. The girls on the team were players that I looked up to because I wanted to play as well as they did.

That year, our team was undefeated not only in our league, but in our area, beating out a select team that I now play for. For a kid that never played before I thought it was the most amazing experience. Even though I was the newest member of an existing team, I worked very hard to contribute in any way I could. I knew that there was so much more that I could do with more training and I was committed to learning as much as I could.

Our team split up that year after an amazing season. A select group of girls were moving up and I was not asked to go with them to a new team. It left me devastated. I know it hurt my coach just as much to have to tell me. Here we were winning the championship game on a weekend that the heat was well over 100 degrees, working so hard to get the hardware, only to have a trophy presented and five minutes later I was a player with no team.

I could have let that defeat me. I could have chosen to never play again. I am not going to hide the fact that I was crushed, because I was and I began to make all kinds of excuses like I was the newest player, I was not good enough to move up, I was not the most popular girl on the team. Yes, I thought them all.

But I respected my coach (and he is still one of my favorites). And I knew at that very moment I was not going to make excuses for the change. I was going to be the best player and allow them to see how dedicated I was to this sport they had introduced me to. So that day I began my journey. Seeking out excellence in my sport.

Expect Excellence of Yourself and Others

It all starts by accepting nothing but the best from yourself. You have to be committed to personal excellence and growth. On one of my mentor sessions I had with coach Jenn she said just concentrate on "Being your best self and live your best life". I strive to live by that motto every single day.

Just simply lose the excuses. Start where you are. Use what you've got and live the life you want!

When you find something that you are passionate about it tends to be easier because you are following your heart. Life is just too short to spend it doing something you don't love. That does not mean it's always going to be easy.

Remember:

"If it does not challenge you, it doesn't change you!"

If what you are doing right now is not your passion, then what in the world do you have to lose? For me softball is a lifestyle. It's more than a sport.

Finding excellence means you have to stop making excuses of why you can't do something and replace it by what you are willing to do. By taking action, getting feedback from others you are not only expanding your knowledge you are increasing your opportunities. Remember, you might get lucky and stumble on an opportunity, but sometimes those only happen once in a lifetime. Mostly, you just have to go out and work hard for what you want.

Choosing Excellence in Others

When looking for excellence, many things you want to know have already been experienced firsthand by others that share in your passion. I have found that I can achieve so much more by studying what others have already done and the steps they took to get there. Building "my house" with the knowledge I gain from them. In the process I keep a journal of best practices and remove everything else.

I was told by a coach to be your best self you need to surround yourself with great athletes and people. Because you are the average of the five people you spend the most time with. (So don't bring down the average by spending lots of time with those that will throw you off your journey for excellence).

Choosing Excellence in Effort

Sports taught me at an early age that there are no shortcuts. **You have to do the work.** You have to put in the effort. You have to have the focus. And when you fall, you have to get back up and go at it again, and again, and again.

By learning this, each time I have taken the mound, it gets a little easier. I get more confident. Being an athlete means making a habit out of excellence. And by making habits out of the very things that make excellence possible.

For me that was a demanding practice schedule, coaches who hold me to the highest of expectations, the same expectations that they hold for themselves. And by them leading by example it encourages me to do the same.

When striving for excellence, you have to lose the excuses like *"I might fail"* - It's entirely possible – but, so what? In fact, it's inevitable. Instead of making excuses, change the way you look at what you call "failure". If it teaches you something about yourself, if you learn something from it, or if it directs you in another path, then it's not failure. No need for excuses. You are on a path of excellence because you are learning.

There are many ways to live a life of excellence. By working hard and not making excuses your potential is limitless. I know that I have personally made some accomplishments, one is in writing this book. However, I am nowhere near where I envision myself in the future. And I know that by using the keys and building my house and character that I will always find room for personal growth.

Here are a few ways that will help guide you in living a life of excellence.

- **Discover Your Purpose**
  Create a mission statement for yourself. When you journal (and I do hope you decide to start) you will discover and be able to craft your own mission statement. Mine is, *"Touch other's lives, be a leader and through my actions help others achieve to live their best life in doing what they love".*

- **Follow Your Passion**
  To do what you love is truly the only way to be happy.

- **Set Your Goals**
  What are your goals and dreams? Set them. If not you are going to find yourself running in place and getting nowhere.

- **Journal (yes Journal!)**
  Again, the power in this will help you with goals, dreams, plans, values and other things that are important to you

and if used a guide to get you there.

- **List of Goals**
  Make a list of the things that you want to accomplish in your journal and create steps to make it happen. Use your S.M.A.R.T goals. For everyone you accomplish add a new one. Never stop growing and learning!

- **Good Attitude**
  The quality of your life is determined by the quality of your thoughts. No one can stop you with the right attitude.

- **Get Mentors**
  When you have big dreams and big visions there will always be people that have done it before you. Look for those that can mentor you and who can unlock your potential for you to achieve so much more. Personally, my mentor has been instrumental in putting structure and meaning to my life. The encouragement I get from someone outside of family (family always believes in you) is additional reinforcement that is not bound by blood.

- **Stop Worrying so Much**
  Fears are in our head. Get rid of them and spend your energy on things that are productive.

- **Let Go of Negative Friendships**
  This one was difficult for me. I spent a lot of time trying to be liked by everyone instead of just those that were good for me. I thought that you were defined by how many friends you had, not by the quality of friends you

had. If you have friends that discourage you and pull you down, it's time to distance yourself from them. There could be greater consequences down the road with peer pressure. So instead of wasting time and energy resisting them, focus your energy on the friends and things that make you happy.

- **Surround Yourself with Positive People**
  Spend time with people that inspire you. You will be amazed at the effects that they will have on you.

- **Believe in Yourself**
  My past experiences have taught me that all you need in order to succeed is a belief in yourself and your abilities. It's really as simple as that!

- **Criticize Less, Appreciate More**
  This is almost the same as negative friendships but it's actually the way you look at things. Don't always be so focused on what is wrong with something, or a person's skills that might be less than your own. Learn to see and appreciate what's there instead. Besides it opens other doors for you to be a leader and help someone else and be their mentor if you know they are struggling.

So what are you waiting for? Start working hard. Surround yourself with people that encourage success. Look for those people you look up to and ask them to mentor you and hold you accountable. Choose to live a life of excellence.

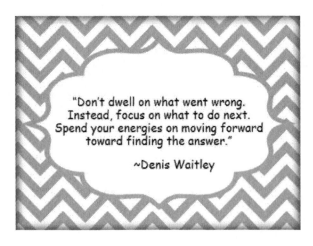

"Don't dwell on what went wrong.
Instead, focus on what to do next.
Spend your energies on moving forward
toward finding the answer."

~Denis Waitley

Chapter Seven

FOCUS ON FORWARD

Mistakes or errors occur every day in the game of softball. I know that sometimes I don't have my mental game in check that allows me to let go of the errors or bad pitches and as a result, I find that if I do not get a handle on the situation that it really hurts my chances for success.

I am sure you have made some mistakes either playing ball or in life, which you were unable to forget quickly. It happens to all of us.

For me, I had a tendency to carry the mistake with me the entire inning or even the rest of the game. I found myself not being able to enjoy the game I love or even the rest of my day because I was too busy beating myself up. But dwelling on the mistake does not help you get the error back, but most definitely will take your head out of the game.

If I was on the mound and was making bad pitches, I found that if I dwelled on the mistakes that it became a distraction the rest of the game. Eventually you forget to be playing in the moment, enjoying the game because your mind is just stuck on a bad pitch or play. It was when my teammates would refer to me as a "pouty pitcher" that I realized, I was not just affecting my game but theirs.

Once you start dwelling on an error or bad pitch, it is very hard to stop the negativity. And you end up spending so much time trying to avoid making an error or bad pitch that you are no longer focusing on just playing the game.

I have attended several softball camps from some of my "softball idols". The common phrase used was "one pitch at a time" and "believe in yourself". Now if the greats of our time like Jennie Finch, Monica Abbott and Cat Osterman are still feeling the same as I do, and still fight with the little negativity in their heads, I assume it will always be there, as well as in mine.

So the key is "Focus on Forward". If the best in the game are able to let go of mistakes and learn from them, I know that we can as well. We have to use the mistakes to help us grow and become better softball players. The key is to learn to let go of mistakes quickly and maintain focus so that it does not snowball and affect the next pitch or play, and by doing so we become a better player. If you're like me and struggle with letting go of the mistakes, don't expect your mental game to change overnight. Like your skills on the mound, it takes time and practice.

Choose to Focus on the Next Play

The first thing an athlete needs to understand is that we are playing a game that you will fail the majority of the time. In softball, the average college player literally fails about six or seven out of the 10 times at bat – and that's considered good!

So when we expect to perform perfectly or have a zero-mistake performance, you are actually setting yourself up for failure. Because in that moment, when the mistake is made, you think you are under performing.

So to "Focus on Forward" your first step is to be mentally prepared and know that athletes make mistakes and you just have to accept this fact.

The second step is to manage the expectations that cause

you to "check-out" and sometimes give up when you make a bad play.

You have to be willing to accept mistakes. Be mindful of the expectations that set you up for feeling like you are failing.

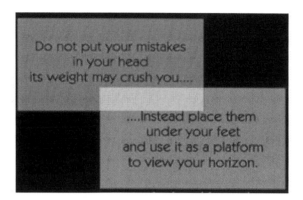

There will always be an *"off-day"* where everything seems to just not work as planned. It's so easy to focus on what went wrong and put all of our focus on the mistake. But learn from those mistakes, let them become the things that push you to grow. Change the event to something we can learn from, making us better athletes, not breaking us down.

Practice the 3 P's of Mental Toughness

- Present – One pitch- One play and forget about it!
- Process - Play like you were trained
- Positive – Stay positive
-

We all must understand that it takes failure and the ability to bounce back. As athletes we develop mental toughness through our failures. As much as our parents do not want us to fail and try to protect us from failures, as I have said before...That is how we learn.

"Every strikeout got me closer to my next homerun".
~ Babe Ruth

Did you know that Babe Ruth grew up in
an orphanage? During his playing career he struck
out a record 1330 times on his way to hitting 714
career homeruns.

Your performance in a game or scoring of a dreaded test
at school can be a devastating disappointment. When things
don't turn out the way that you had hoped for, sometimes it
can be so easy to blame everything except how you might be
handling the situation.

Take 100% Responsibility for Your Emotions

Personally, when I decided to start taking responsibility for
my negative feelings, and not react to my disappointment, I
realized how easy it is to rise above it. I am not going to tell
you it was an easy transition, and there are times that I still
need to work on it. But once you can leave that place of
disappointment and move forward it feels like a weight has
been lifted off of your shoulders.

If you've been disappointed, here's a few things you can
try to rise above your negative feelings, and avoid
disappointment in the future.

- **Define Your Expectations**
  There will be times when something occurs that
  allows you to be disappointed. Just take a deep
  breath and try to determine the real cause to that
  disappointment. Could it be that you did not
  practice enough and were not prepared? Or
  could your expectations not have been met even
  under the best of circumstances? Once you can
  define the true issue, you are already taking steps

66

to better deal with it, instead of letting it destroy you.

- **Be Okay to Feel How You Feel**
  Sometimes we may feel discouraged and disappointed. That is okay. If we pretend that everything is okay, it won't make the situation any better so just take control and accept your feelings, and they won't control you.

- **Practice Gratitude**
  Practice gratitude for the things that went right instead of things that might have gone wrong. Help yourself to pick out the good and positive things in the game instead of dwelling on the negatives.

- **Learn from Your Experience**
  Depending on what your expectations were, you have the ability to change it the next time. Remember focus on forward, learn from it.

"The most important thing in communication is hearing what isn't being said."

~Unknown

Chapter Eight

COMMUNICATION CHANGES THE GAME

There are so many different ways to communicate these days. Being twelve, I have never known a time any different than email, Twitter, Facebook, or Instagram just to name a few. Social media is everywhere.

But communication on the field in sports is more important than ever. Not only do your coaches need to communicate their expectations, but good communication is an important part of your team's performance and growth on and off the field.

In softball, communication is key! Our goal is to first, avoid collision so that we can avoid injury. And second, ensure that all of our plays are made, nobody gets hurt, and everyone knows where everyone else is on the field. When communication is present on a team, you begin to develop trust in one another, resulting in a winning and successful team!

Communication between teammates is important in a game. But communication goes beyond that. It starts at practice and in the dugout.

Communication can be something verbal and non-verbal. Think about how you feel when a teammate gives you a *"high-five"* after an at bat. Does not matter if you went down swinging. What mattered is the communication they gave you following that allows you to focus on forward.

What Great Communication Looks Like

If you were to tell your team mates *"Good Job", "Great at Bat"* then you are communicating a positive message, in what can sometimes be a self-defeating moment that might just turn it around. Good team communication can sometimes be the difference in winning and losing in a game.

If you want to have an effective team then you will need to learn to work together. Everyone should do their part in building strong relationships amongst the members.

I find that the time we do our off the field team bonding is where I learn more about my teammates. We talk about past experiences, things we like to do during our down time and it really helps everyone know their teammates better. I believe that spending quality "bonding time" and communicating at a personal level makes for easier communication and trust on the field.

Communicating as a Leader

Communication needs to be something that starts with the coaches. As a leader you can model this too. An effort should be made to work with your team to establish ground rules and work to bring the team together so that they can accomplish their goals. As an athlete you can also help open up communication with your coach by sharing your needs.

When team communication skills are strong, then every member becomes a contributor with confidence instead of being a team member that is hesitant to provide input for the fear of being criticized or having their ideas laughed at.

I found that the best coaches I have had will take the extra time following games to have each player communicate one positive thing about each player for the game.

It served two purposes. One it kept us alert and paying attention throughout the game and learning through game play, and secondly, allowed us to help celebrate even the smallest of accomplishments in the game. We all look forward to the "Kudos" from our teammates. We work harder in the process, especially once we hear that not only did they realize the accomplishments we all made, but that they took mental note enough to share with the team following the game. Win or lose...we felt good about our efforts.

There are four areas of communication that are important to any team:

- **On The Field– (Where you perform)**
  In softball, unlike individual played sports, you rely on your training, but you also have to communicate to your team members. You can do this by calling the number of outs, or where the next play is or if you are calling a ball. On field communication is important when going for a ball so that your teammate backs off from the play when you have made the call. Team on field chatter also helps the team to stay in the game and focused on the plays.

- **Non-Verbal**
  No doubt your coaches have taught you a series of signs that indicate what you need to do at an at bat or play on the field. Every team member has memorized every possible signal and ensuring that the signals are complicated and varied enough so that the other team can't pick up on them easily. Communication by signaling is extremely important.

- **In The Dugout– (Where you prepare with your team)**
  Motivation and encouragement by far the most important thing that your teammates can contribute

when in the dugout. I can tell you the difference in the games I have played where you have 12 girls rallying, cheering and pumping up their team and letting your opponent know that you are not giving up. That you are going to go down fighting and giving 100% no matter what the score is. The excitement, passion and support of your teammates it shows them that you believe in them, it shows you support them and as softball sisters it shows that you love them. So when you hear your coach say *"Get off the bench!"*, do it. Get to the fence, and give it everything you got. See the difference it will make.

- **And After the Game-(Winners and losers in a game)** Sometimes you will be the on the losing side of the equation. The sooner you accept this, the easier it is to handle a loss. When you lose, don't pout, throw a temper tantrum or blame your teammates or the umpires. If you are giving the game 100% and leaving it on the field then there is no shame in a loss. So don't show your opponents a weakness or embarrass your parents by bad behavior. Just learn from it and accept the loss.

  But if you find yourself with the win. Remember to show some class. Don't gloat or put down the other team after your win. The best way to earn respect in our game is that after a win you take the time to tell the other team *"good game"*. Perhaps even offer some compliments to a player or their coach for a play they made.

How You Communicate is always a Choice.

I had once played for a team that was a good team, but followed the lead of another player who was upset after a game for getting out. We had actually won the game and the other

72

team created a tunnel to walk through to celebrate our victory, even though they had lost. One of the girls made the comment *"Don't go through their tunnel"* and all of the girls followed suit. Thinking it was funny, and quickly found out how hurtful it really was.

Not only did the team look bad, we had embarrassed our coach who quickly had us back on the other side of the field to apologize to the coaches, the team and the parents as well as the umpires for the behavior of the team. It was at that moment that I realized that we had communicated to all those at the ballpark our lack of sportsmanship. We communicated that day that we had no respect for our coaches, our team or our parents.

That was a hard day that I am still not proud of, but one we all learned from. Communication can change the game. How you communicate in every situation can set a perception of yourself and your team.

Great teams are not formed overnight. But one thing that I notice on the field is that the best teams have great coaches that communicate well with their teams, setting an example and making them accountable. And I'm so thankful that I do not have a coach that would allow that type of behavior.

Having good communication skills is really important off the field as well. By practicing these things in your day to day life it can help you develop your skills to better communicate with teachers, parents and members of your community.

"Communication is what makes a team strong".
~Brian McClennan

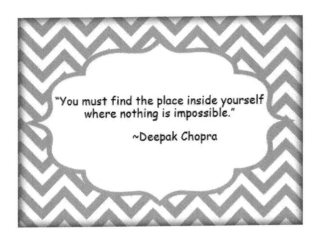

"You must find the place inside yourself
where nothing is impossible."

~Deepak Chopra

Chapter Nine

UNLEASH YOUR INNER WARRIOR

There are some days, I feel like a "warrior-princess" on the mound. Before I even hustle out to the circle, my attitude of confidence fuels my desire to perform successfully.

Inner determination I believe is important in sports. As athletes we should always want to strive to push ourselves beyond the normal limitations that we set for ourselves. We all have a warrior spirit. It's the desire to be competitive.

Sometimes that warrior spirit is not realized until you are placed in a situation that pushes you to reach deeper, play harder than any time before. But just imagine if we lived our lives in a way that this was what we strived for everyday in every aspect of our lives.

> "Fight for your dreams. JUST DO IT.
>
> Leave it all on the field"
>
> ~Billy Cox

Having a "warrior spirit" is an attitude. It's having the conviction to do everything to the utmost of your ability. It does not matter if its training, doing your homework or simply doing your chores that you don't like. You always do your best because that is who you are, not because there is a reward for doing it. Even though the rewards do come.

75

Having a warrior spirit on the field playing a sport you love is willingness to train your body, mind and inner spirit not just at a minimum requirement. You must be willing to pursue every task at the highest level. There is no greater feeling than to have approached your sport with 100% effort and commitment. When you work hard and encourage your teammates to do the same by always trying to better yourselves together.

So what does it take to possess a warrior spirit?

- **100% Effort and Commitment in All You Do.**
  Being a warrior means you give it 100% every day.
  That is what makes you a fierce warrior and sets you apart from your competition on and off the field.

- **Always Looks for Ways to Grow**
  A warrior looks for every opportunity to learn
  and put that knowledge to work.

- **Takes Responsibility for All Actions**
  Being a warrior means being responsible for the choices
  and decisions that you make, even when it makes you
  uncomfortable for owning up to a bad one.

- **Always Be True to Yourself**
  Have a fighting spirit always brave enough
  to stand-up for yourself and not to go with
  the herd over peer pressure. Do what you
  know is right and always protect your heart
  and integrity.

- **Always Train Mind, Body and Spirit for Growth**
  A warrior always trains, never missing an opportunity
  to grow in mind, body and spirit.

Being the best version of yourself is not only exceeding your performance on the field, but it also includes eating right and getting enough sleep. These things help you with your overall performance.

I am sure that you have heard people say that if you see it you can achieve it. Well I do believe that is true. Sometimes I take a few minutes before stepping to the circle and just close my eyes, get really relaxed and see myself making the pitch. If I start that process before I even take to the field visualizing the success, then I strive to recreate the vision in my head. Now I won't have the time to do this with every pitch, but if I do it before I go in, it brings a sense of peace to at least start the game and a good way to develop your inner warrior.

Mental Imagery

Mental Imagery involves the athlete imagining themselves performing a specific activity. The images should have the athlete performing this task **very well** and **successfully**

Some of us are already warriors in one form or another. Having that warrior mindset just means you won't quit. You play every game like your life depends on it.

Having a warrior mindset is really about confidence in your abilities. Your "Yes, I can do it" warrior attitude helps you take a definite charge of your future. A positive "warrior sprit" helps control every step of your progress.

Being able to bring out your "warrior spirit" enables you to create a strong belief in your ability to cope with whatever life may bring. You'll always be positive and ready to take on anything. Having a warrior mindset will allow you to find opportunities in difficult problems or situations and will push you so that you will never be defeated for trying your best. No challenge will be too big.

Any skill on the field or class in school can be learned by little difficulty if you have the proper attitude.

To help you bring out your inner warrior and develop a "Can- Do" attitude try these tips:

- **Have a "Can-Do" Attitude**
  Always believe in your abilities. A warrior is not afraid to go after what they want. Don't just think you can do it....know you can do it....and don't stop until it has been achieved.

- **Be a Person of Integrity**
  Think, talk, act, and conduct yourself in a way to be the person you want to be and that your future self will thank you for!

- **Make a Difference**
  When you go after something you want to achieve, let it be something that makes a difference. It could be your sport, your studies, your community or something to help you grow. Just make it meaningful.

- **Always Look for Opportunities**
  Having a warrior sprit will drive you to always look for an opportunity for growth. If you come across a problem, just face it as a challenge and look for the opportunities within.

- **Go Outside of Your Comfort Zone**
  Try something different that challenges you. Keep trying new things until you succeed. Don't ever give up!

> "The spirit of a warrior resides with YOU!".
>
> ~Unknown

All of the keys in this book help build that warrior spirit that you have. Everything builds upon one another to develop you in preparation and belief in accomplishing great things whether it be on the field or in your personal life.

"It's not how **good** you are,

It's how **good** you want to be."

~Paul Arden

Chapter Ten

CHALLENGE YOURSELF TO MORE THAN AVERAGE

I am not so convinced that there are natural born athletes. While I would agree that some of us are more athletic than others, the truth of the matter is that if you want to be good at something or great at something it takes work.

We all have potential to be extraordinary in sports and in life. But it wasn't until I had a mentor share with me the *"play-up principle"* that I started to realize I had the power to determine the outcome of everything that I wanted to accomplish.

Every year at tryouts, I over hear parents boasting to their friends or other parents that their child is going to *"play-up"* because they are so much better than someone else. But really, that is not the kind of "playing-up" I am referring to although it is close to the same experience.

Everyone starts at the same place when they start anything. Some of us have an advantage because we were raised in the environment that wants to excel in, whatever that *"thing"* is.

> **"The expert in anything was once a beginner".**
>
> **~Helen Hays**

Playing-up is a way to challenge you to do more than average. If you want to improve your skills at whatever you are trying to achieve it's more than just showing up. Anyone can do that.

In my experience playing softball it's not just about your performance, it's also about you making the most of your talent and potential. You need to always look for ways to highlight your strengths and dedication to your sport by hustling and constantly competing. Every time you have a practice or game you are making an impression. It could be to a coach, a parent or a softball player that is looking up to you.

My curveball or changeup may not show up every day, but effort and passion can. A strong passion for the game will help you get better quickly. It can also catch the attention of coaches who are always on the lookout for dedicated players who can be transformed in to high school and college athletes.

You Were Gifted With Potential

I believe that we are all created to be amazing, but we were also created to grow. And when we are not growing or learning you are declining. By that I mean if you just do the same old thing every day, it becomes just routine and you become less motivated, less effective and less optimistic.

To become more than average it means taking the time to invest in yourself to grow and improve. At the beginning of the book I said that everyone has God-given potential to do great things, but many of us never realize that potential because they do not know how.

In sports there are many athletes that have set examples for us. Find a mentor in whatever skill you want to improve. It could be for a Math or English class, of someone that plays college ball. It could be someone on your team that possesses the skills that you want to achieve. But go to them.

As an athlete, you already have the mindset to accomplish a lot, but no matter what, you will always be limited by your available time and experience. Being able to learn from other people's experiences, wisdom and skills is a way to kick-start your growth and capabilities.

Mentors Matter

The mentors who I have been lucky enough to work with have been valuable to me helping me move forward, take initiative and untangle the many challenges I am faced with. I have several mentors that I call on. I have one that I go to for spiritual growth, one for sports and athletic guidance and one that is all encompassing and I am proud to call my life coach.

Mentors will offer guidance when you are trying to figure out how to solve a problem. They provide motivation when you begin to *"lose steam"* and need someone to help push you forward to obtain your goal. My life coach and mentor Jenn Starkey has shared connections within her own network that has introduced me to opportunities that have allowed me to grow much quicker than I think I could have ever done on my own.

So this key in building yourself is extremely important. If you can get someone else to contribute a little bit of their experience and add it to your own enthusiastic dreams and goals, you will leapfrog past many of the obstacles that slow others down. In just going the extra mile in this one area, you become more than average. In short, mentors are vital.

In general people love to share what they've learned with others, especially young people. So don't be shy in asking for advice of help, but make sure you respect their time. Most people that you ask would consider it an honor to be asked to help someone. That is also showing them that their hard work is being noticed and validates all of the efforts that they have put into their skill. Playing-up is just making you stretch to a harder level. Remember, *"If it does not challenge you, it does not change you"* and playing-up allows you to put this into action.

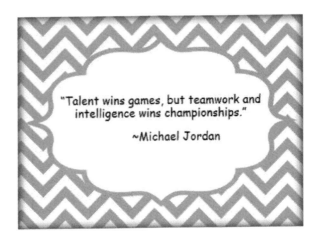

"Talent wins games, but teamwork and intelligence wins championships."

~Michael Jordan

Chapter Eleven

NEVER UNDERESTIMATE THE POWER OF A TEAM

I have been very fortunate to have played for some great coaches that have built great teams. Having a group of teammates that are working towards the same goal is important because achieving the victories almost always requires the effort of every team member, even those cheering from the dugout are important.

Every player relies on their teammates to perform to the best of their ability. All possess different skills and strengths. But together, they are like a well-oiled machine.

No team is successful without working together to reach a common goal. When playing sports it's important to treat your teammates with respect. Cooperating with each other and putting aside any differences that you might have for the greater good of the team.

Teamwork doesn't just happen. It needs to be built. When you are playing a sport like softball, it helps to have good coaching. A coach will manage the team's development and work on player's individual strengths. Their job is to focus on identifying where an individual athletes best contribution on the team can be made.

A team needs to have faith in their coach. I have been playing softball for 5 years. I know that I like to play several key positions. But ultimately it's up to the coach to assign a position and it's up to me to work hard and earn the position that I want.

A successful team requires trust. Trust will allow each team member to depend on each other. When trust is lacking, the members play as individuals, weakening the whole team. I have to admit, I have been part of a team this has happened to. I typically pitch, and because I had lack of trust of my team members because I did not feel that they put as much into the work as I was that I started playing the whole infield myself. I would find that I was getting so frustrated that my game was no better than the fear I had of them not being able to perform.

I am not proud of that, but it made me realize that to have a strong team, you must trust. Trust is built when your team members get to know each other and their abilities and commitment. It grows as the team practices together enough that the team has developed an instinctive feel for one another.

When the 12 girls on the team begin to share the same enthusiasm that is born out of the desire to be a contributing member of the team, shared ambition to be the best, gives the team direction. When a team is united in their quest for the same goal they are unstoppable.

It all starts with everyone showing up for practice, giving 100% every practice. Teammates that just "go through the motions" without motivation will eventually cripple the team. So as a team, it's everyone's job to include, motivate and encourage your softball sisters to achieve.

> "The strength of the team is each individual member...the strength of each member is the team!" ~Phil Jackson

Finally, there is one element that makes a team great, beyond teamwork. It's simply "team chemistry" though it's really more than that. You can have a great team with great skills who have excellent teamwork skills. You have to work on building your team with trust, communication and respect. That is the kind of chemistry that makes a team thrive and without it simply fall apart.

But I think the best teams are those that enjoy being together. More than just softball players with talent, but great people as well. They have confidence in themselves and in their teammates that the job will get done. No matter what the game situation, great teams know they can handle it. Win or lose they come out better from the experience.

Recently, I guest played on a middle school team and they did something that I thought was really a great way to get the girls to know more about each other. Especially since we all knew very little other than we all loved softball.

All of us were in the outfield and the coach was hitting fly balls to each of us. When we caught the ball, we had to reveal a little-known fact about ourselves before we could release the ball. If the play was in the outfield, then the athlete would throw the ball to an infield player, who would also have to share a fact about themselves. The infield player then returned the ball to the coach. The coach would then state his expectations of the team. And in that process we all had a sense of trust and "sisterhood" while working on our essential catching and throwing skills. It was a great way to break the ice and make us comfortable working together as a team.

There are lots of ways to build great teams. Here are a few suggestions that have helped me feel part of a team that has that special chemistry.

- Know each other as people, not just teammates on the field. We are all more than just the uniforms we wear. It may not always be possible to hang out all of the time with every member of the team, but do try to get to know each other outside of the ballpark. You will find they will be your biggest supporter years to come. Cherish them as friends and teammates.

- Be a leader. That does not mean put yourself in a higher position than them. It means always be a leader, sharing and encouraging growth. Everyone on the team has different strengths and weaknesses. Help others where they need help and encouragement, and get with someone that will help you.
- If you have rules within your team always connect them to a value. That way, everyone understands the need to have the rules and will support and respect them.
- Respond to misunderstandings. Always start with the assumption that your teammates had positive intentions.
- Recognize that teams are stronger when you respect each other for their different skill levels and viewpoints. Who wants to be on a team of clones?
- Respect and encourage your softball sister's viewpoints. Allow everyone to explain their point of view instead of knocking it.
- Always give each other positive feedback. *"Great at Bat!"* regardless of the outcome. *"Wasn't your time, next time!"* Uncertainty feeds fear, and fear erodes trust within a team. Let them know that it's ok, there is always next time. Keep encouraging.

Most important is to remember to work hard as a team, and play well together. And every time you are together it's an opportunity to make a memory! **Make your time count!**

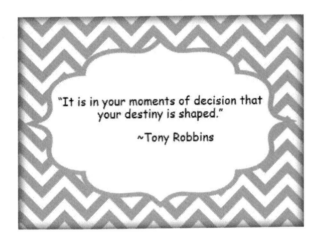

"It is in your moments of decision that your destiny is shaped."

~Tony Robbins

Chapter Twelve

YOUR DECISIONS DETERMINE YOUR DESTINY

For me, this was one of the most difficult chapters to write. But as a young athlete I feel that it is important and something that we all need to be aware of.

If you are reading this book, you no doubt have a love of this sport, you have an interest in working hard and being the best that you can be. I am hoping in some small way that you have found the information helpful.

Choices to be Aware of

If you are like me and looking forward to what lies ahead in your life, it is not too early to consider the things that will come around and rob you of all of the efforts.

I have been fortunate enough to have had exposure to many athletes, both at a college and professional level that have had very frank conversations with me and others about the dangers of social media, alcohol, drugs and peer-pressure.

Choices and Social Media

I believe that as young people it is a great way of getting our messages out in the world as well as learning some really cool things. But like all things, there is a limit to the goodness it brings and always a dark and sinister side that needs to be addressed.

We have discussed the importance of working hard, pushing yourself to a higher standard. Perhaps, it's just to do your best at all things. It could be to earn a scholarship through academics and sports.

Athletes need to have responsible behavior at all times. They need to be very much aware of the risks they take by participating in sites like Facebook and Twitter and how quickly something can be posted that can cause problems for their team or themselves.

It could be a tweet about a coach, a teacher an opponent or a teammate that feasters into a tense situation at a game.

Just because you think the messages are not being monitored except by your friends, that could be no further from the truth. College coaches are the ones that are monitoring Twitter and Facebook accounts more than your friends. You can work hard on the field for years and get the coveted scholarship and by just one random incident caused by posting a questionable photo or inappropriate message can hurt you image-wise. It can lead to jealousy or resentment from your teammates.

Anything that you put on the internet is out there, there is no room for error and you can't take it back. Most do not realize it until it's too late. Bad social media posts might mean whether or not a college offers you a scholarship.

We all tend to be so reactionary to what people post, sometimes we just join in on whatever rant is going on in the group. That can be so dangerous. Your words can come back and bite you, even if they were not meant to harm. And people that you think are your friends, may spread something you post to others not in the group by a simple capture of your screen. I discussed the very issue with my pitching coach. He is always good about letting his pitchers know what they stand to lose by being reckless with our thoughts and words. Below is what was shared:

"I have seen the power of social media destroy player's careers and destroy teams. Placing derogatory comments about teammates or coaches can alienate the player posting the comment as well as the player it was about as well as kill the team chemistry. If you are truly TEAM oriented then nothing negative should ever be posted where teammates, coaches or the general public should be able to see it. Also, we are not always judged by who we are but by how others see us and your conduct on social media can greatly affect you negatively. Here's a good example....A former college player (sophomore at the time and still under age) placed pictures on her public Facebook page showing her drinking illegally and obviously intoxicated. Recruits were brought in for overnight visits and met her and then friended her on Facebook. A parent of one of the recruits saw the pictures and brought it to the coach's attention while telling him why her daughter was no longer interested in that softball program. She was suspended from the team for 30 days and then demoted to the JV team. The consequences of what you place on social media can be far reaching."

-Jim Griener, Griener Fastpitch
Owner and Pitching Instructor and Softball Clinician
College Softball Coach, Lindenwood University

In this example, it was not just the girl that was involved that was affected, but a girl being recruited, whom no longer wanted to be a part of that softball program. The athlete's perceived harmless activity not only affected her, but also tarnished another from wanting to be part of a sport that we all are trying to grow.

I am thankful that I have constant reminders from my coaches of how important our actions and decisions are. Although speaking your mind is something you are entitled to, it is something that you must be cautious of.

I had attended a NCAA Softball camp last year in Oklahoma City where I had the privilege of speaking with Coaches Mickey Dean, Head Coach of the James Madison Softball Program and Coach Marla Townsend, Head Coach of University of Alabama at Birmingham. They discussed the recruiting process and the types of athletes that they tend to look for and those that they do not consider.

Both stated that *"if there's a lot of questionable stuff that they're posting, even if they have talent, they would stop recruiting the athlete"*

Researching potential college athletes by way of social media has become the norm across the nation, ranging from Junior college to Division 1 athletic programs.

"So, if you're even near qualifying for a scholarship that can save you thousands of dollars on a college degree and provide you the opportunity to excel as an athlete in a great program, be careful on social media"

So be smart and don't post something that you will

regret costing you everything that you have worked for and the sacrifices that both you and your family have made for the opportunity to play college sports.

Here are a few things to consider if you use social media that perhaps will help you decide what kinds of things that you should or should not post.

- If you wouldn't want your grandmother to see it then **DON'T** post it.

- If you even hesitated for a second to post it, DON'T. There is a reason you hesitated in the first place.

- Make sure that your default picture (and all others) are appropriate.

- Privacy settings only work so far. Social media is public, always keep that in mind.

- Respect yourself and respect others. Social media is a public platform after all.

- Even if you did not originate the tweet or post, once you post to it, it's no different than if you posted it yourself.

- If you do not like something someone wrote about you, your coach or your teammate, ignore it. Engaging in a public Twitter or Facebook argument is a battle you will not win.

- Act as a representative of your sport and team and always maintain a professional profile.

Choices on Alcohol, Drugs & Peer Pressure

When we think about our choices, even the *"just once"* ones, I don't think we ever consider what those choices cost us.

Too many times have I heard the stories from my coaches of a player that made a bad decision either by drinking and getting behind the wheel, or getting involved by taking what is *"perceived"* as a harmless drug that *"one-time"* experience can cost you the most ultimate of a price.

Youth today are making choices that are affecting their lives and their families' lives causing tragedy. It makes me sad because the instances I have been exposed to, were all good people, good athletes with lots of talent and loving, caring people. Making a bad choice for whatever reason.

They are making choices to put the things that they have sacrificed for on the line, to make a choice with the intention of *"harmless fun"*, or in the hopes to fit in with others.

This happens every day to athletes and people who you would never expect intelligent, loving and caring individuals with hope and promise. They make a bad choice because of the fear of failure, the stress they feel and the hope to feel better.

They often loose it all, and in some cases even their life in a moment when they weren't thinking about the possible consequences of the choice they were about to make.

I just want each of you to know, **YOU ARE IMPORTANT**. The contributions you will make are important. Remember to make good choices and when you are facing a tough time imagine a bright future, people you can lift up with your story. **Your life is valuable.**

JUST REMEMBER……

Regardless of what you are experiencing in life, God is with you. Let this Psalm bring a comfort and reminder that he is ever present and aware of your problems and needs. **You are loved!**

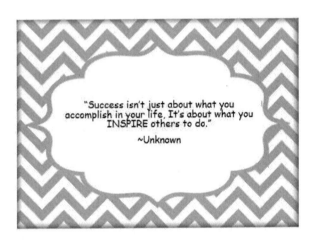

"Success isn't just about what you accomplish in your life, It's about what you INSPIRE others to do."

~Unknown

Chapter Thirteen

INSPIRE others with your story

Well you made it through the book. The thirteenth key.

Live by choice, not by chance. Make changes, not excuses. Be motivated, not manipulated. Work to excel, not just to compete. Listen to your own inner voice, not the jumbled opinions of everyone else that are not going the same direction that you are.

How can you use all of these tools to grow into the best version of you? Use what you learn through the choices you make to inspire others.

You can choose to follow the herd where everyone is trying to make you like everyone else, or you can find the courage to follow that inner voice that reminds you to dream and keep being your awesome self. Embrace everything you are about, your ideas and strengths and weaknesses. Be the person that you know you were meant to be. The best version of you!

> "If you cannot put your heart in it,
>
> take yourself out of it."
>
> ~Unknown

Just remember coaches, teammates, teachers and friends watch what you do more than they listen to what you say. Lead by your good choices. Be someone worth being admired. People follow people that they can respect and look up to. That is why I chose to have a mentor and why I recommend that you find one to help you in your life.

> "People will rarely remember what you did, but they will always remember how you made them feel"
>
> ~Maya Angelou

Make the reputation for yourself that is known for personal excellence. And although a reputation is important, know that your character is who you really are. A person of good moral character always outshines and inspires others.

Practice every day your values. Walk the talk!

> "Be the change you want to see in the world"
>
> ~Mahatma Gandhi

Just as my mentors and coaches have challenged me, I challenge you. Be the friend that inspires others to be what you know that they can be. Sometimes it takes someone to just let them know that you believe that they have great potential and expect great things from them. Be the mentor to help them along.

Most often the friends or teammates that look up to you will go to great lengths to live up to the expectations once they know someone is willing to stand beside them and make the journey with them. Be that friend.

Start noticing what you like about others. Go out of your way to pass that team motivation to all of those around you and complement those that are working hard to better themselves. Let them know that it's being noticed. I can tell you from my own experience how good it makes me feel when my mentors or coaches compliment me on improvements that I am making.

Make the choice to be the one to remind others their circumstances do not define them or what they are capable of. You have the power to inspire others. You already inspire me.

- Love Kyleigh.

Acknowledgements

God gives each and every one of us the gift of life.
What we do with that life is our gift back to him.
Thank you God for providing me the strength to rise
above the challenges I face and believing in me and
allowing me to do the things I love with purpose.

I wish to personally thank the following people for their contributions to my inspiration and knowledge and other help in creating this book:

My Grandparents: I love you and thank you for all of the ways you show me unconditional love. You have taught me to live out my dreams. You offer encouragement every day that allows me to do the things I love. I have been blessed because you have supported my dreams and helped me take my journal notes and put them into this book so that I could share with others. I love you both so very much. And no one could love me more!

Samantha and Jonathan Toledo: Thank you so much for always being there for me. Always pushing me to my personal best, always believing in me and encouraging me by your example of the Godly way I should go. Thank You.

To My Mentor Coach Jenn Starkey: Thank you for all of the times you have encouraged, inspired and made me accountable for the things I want to accomplish. I can always count on you for a path to success The countless hours you have worked with me, helping me create " a plan" to successfully reach my dreams. I am so fortunate to be part of your team!

To My Coaches: Thank you for all of the time invested in me to become the best that I can be, especially when I could not see it for myself. Thank you for always believing in me and pushing me to be my best. You never gave up, you just found a new way to get me where I needed to be. You gave me something that I hold very dear. And that is a love of this sport. Each of you have played an important part in my life that I will always treasure. Thank You to Jim Griener, Mickey Debold, Mark Mudd, Joe Dorlac, Lisa Rawlings, Holly Snyder, Marc Stichling and the coach that started it all, Brian Traylor. Each of you have impacted my life in the most rewarding ways. Thank you for sharing your love of the game, and continue to show me how to *"play-up"* to be better with every opportunity.

To My Medical Team: I want to express my thanks and appreciation for all of the wonderful treatment and care that you all show me. When my medical journey started I was nervous and daunted by the fear of the unknown. All of you have demonstrated total commitment to my care. So *"Thank You"* to the staff at St Louis Children's Hospital, Dr. David Molter, Tyler Robertson and Receptionist Lisa Burress who have made my monthly surgeries something I look forward to because of your kindness and compassion. You have encouraged me in my book writing efforts and have made this journey something greater than ever imagined.

Tom and Gina Birkemeier: I have always admired the way that you make me feel special and loved, and how you glorify God by caring for others. My heart has always been drawn to you because I can always feel the love that comes through your actions; spoken or unspoken. You will always be special in my heart. God put you in my path since birth. I am so blessed, so grateful and so honored to know you. Thank you for believing in me.

Alan and Debbie Hunter: A very heartfelt *"Thank You"*. It is because of your comments about my first writings that convinced me that I had something to share with the world. You believed in me, and that alone is what finally pushed me to pursue this effort. I want to touch others the way you have touched my heart. I am so blessed that God put you in my life to share my many journeys and accomplishments with you. I love you both.

Special Thanks

Additional thanks goes to those that have supported my efforts and that inspire me every day.

Taylor "RT" Cantillo
Leah O'Brien Amico
Lauren Haeger
Kaylyn Castillo
Jarrod Rogol
Caleb Maddix
Mr & Mrs Jim Smith
Janet Patterson
Linda Schaible
Sandy Hackenwerth
Teammates of St. Louis Extreme 12U-03
My Amazing Teachers and Friends at RSMS

Notes and Credits

1. http://quotinvestigator.com
2. http://www.merriam-webster.com/dictionary
3. http://www.brainyquote.com
4. NIV 2011

Limited Edition Print
Kyleigh Villarreal's MVP 2016 Leadership Project

MVP
MISSION. VALUES. PURPOSE

The ultimate leadership experience designed for the youth athlete

www.MVPLeadershipAcademy.com

For more information on booking a leadership event for your school, church or organization.

support@MVPLA.net
855-808-TEAM

Made in the USA
Middletown, DE
20 June 2019